What do you get when you give ten top designers a big basket of acrylic stamps and set them free to scrap and stamp till their hearts' content? You get this book bursting with ideas to fashion your own fun, versatile and unique embellishments to enhance your projects.

If they aren't already your favorite item in your scrapbooking toolbox, acrylic stamps will soon become your go-to supply when you want to create dazzling pages. They are easy to use, easy to care for, easy to store and so easy to love!

From unique materials you can stamp on and resourceful media you can stamp with to innovative techniques you can use to craft amazing accents, *The Clear Stamp Book* will arm you with tons of inspiration for your creative ventures.

Grab your stamping supplies and keep this book close by as you work and you'll always be inspired to create something *clearly unique.*

intro

Leslie Lightfoot

Cathy Blackstone

Jackie Bonette

The artists of Autumn Leaves

Becky Novacek

Patricia Anderson

Mellette Berezoski

Jamie Waters

Jennifer Johner

Robyn Werlich

Emily Falconbridge

Jennifer Pebbles

Kelli Crowe

Contents

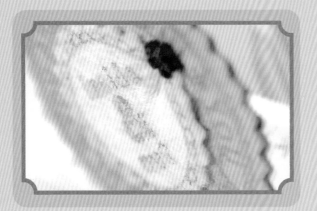

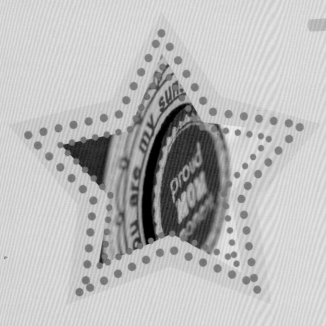

EST. **chapter one**

Materials & Mediums

Imagine if the only books ever written were fiction. We'd miss out on the juicy scoop of biographies and we'd never get to walk in the footsteps of explorers as they discovered new lands. So imagine only stamping with one medium or onto only one material. Our pages and projects would be lackluster if an inkpad and paper were the only materials used. We'd never get to see how cool some images look when stamped on metal, foam or microscope slides. And we wouldn't be impressed with how acrylic ink makes a delightful stamped image, especially when topped with glitter. After reading this chapter, try something *new* to make your projects both **fun** and **beautiful**.

You Glow
By Robyn

Assemble strips of patterned paper to background. Add scalloped border to left side. Zigzag stitch here and there for interest. Adhere enlarged photo and stitch tag and journaling to layout. Paint chipboard initial with pink ink; let dry, then top with clear glitter paint. **Stamp pieces of a cork coaster using paint as the ink.** Embellish with flowers, brads, buttons, string and glitter.

Stamping on Cork

Acrylic stamps and button | AL
Brads | MM and AC
Die cuts | Sizzix
Flowers | Bazzill and AC
Font | AL Serenade
Paint | MM, Delta and DecoArt
Paper | Lasting Impressions, Doodlebug Designs and CI
Pens | Stampin' Up!
Rub-ons | MM

Suburban Moms
By Kelli

Print enlarged photo on paper and tear and ink the edges. Adhere over six 3″ squares of cardstock. **Stamp title letters on various surfaces such as paint chips, stickers, patterned paper, journaling tags, a paper bag, receipt, photo and ticket stub.** When dry, cut out and affix to layout with pop dots.

Acrylic stamps | AL
Ink | Tsukineko
Paper | SEI, AL and KI
Pens | AC
Photo | Rob Darr
Stickers | MM
Tag | 7gypsies

Adoration
By Jamie

Mat two photos on patterned paper. Add ribbon to side and adhere stickers on top. **Stamp title using acrylic paint.** Cut each letter into a rectangle and staple to background. **Stamp additional accent images onto background and finish with small flowers and handwritten journaling.**

Acrylic stamps | AL
Brad | Around the Block
Flowers | Prima
Paper | Fontwerks
Pens | AC
Ribbon | SEI
Stickers | K&Co.

Stamping on Felt

Amazing
By Mellette

Attach strips of floral and dot paper along left side of layout. Add stitching and ribbon on the dot paper. Print title and swirls onto photo and adhere to layout. **Stamp images onto various colors of felt; cut out and layer to create flowers.** Embellish with brads, photo anchors, staples or pins. Machine stitch stems and use as journaling lines.

Digital images | Rhonna Swirls and Swirl Words, www.twopeasinabucket.com
Die cuts, stamps, rub-ons, buttons, brads and ribbon | AL
Font | AL Serenade

Gem stones | Westrim
Ink | Stampin' Up!
Paper | AL
Pens | AC
Software | Adobe Photoshop Elements
Stick pin | MM

Inside of Me
By Mellette

Layer papers on background. Cut half circle from top, back with red and attach die cut inside circle. Print text on photo; mat on black and punch holes along left side. Print journaling on patterned paper. Punch holes down left side, attach clip and adhere next to photo. Cut star border from transparency; secure with staples. Cut metal frame in half diagonally to form large corners. **Using solvent ink, stamp flourishes and star on metal corners and tag;** adhere with mounting tape.

Acrylic stamps, die cuts and transparency | AL
Font | AL Old Style and AL Uncle Charles
Ink | Tsukineko
Metal frame and clip | MM
Metal tag | Nunn Design
Paper | Cherry Arte, Piggy Tale, Chatterbox and Karen Foster
Ribbons | AC
Rub-ons and photo turn | 7gypsies

Baby Rockstar
By Jennifer P.

Create background from various papers. Adhere stars cut from patterned paper. **Stamp journaling lines and apply rub-ons and journaling.** Cut rectangles from foam. With a heat gun, heat for 20 seconds (don't overheat). **Immediately apply stamp to foam, applying strong pressure for 15 seconds.** Lift from foam. Outline inside the image with an opaque white art pen. Secure with clips.

Acrylic stamps | AL
Clips | MM
Ink | Clearsnap
Paper | SEI
Pens | Marvy and Sakura
Ribbon | May Arts
Rub-ons | AC
Trim | Doodlebug Designs

Stamp on a Canvas

This is Love   By Emily

Paint watered-down acrylic paint onto canvas paper. **Create a graffiti look with stamps by layering stamps and colors; start with the lightest color and build up to darker.** Write title on top. Hand stitch around photo.

Acrylic stamps | AL
Paint | Derivan Matisse
Pens | Sharpie

Keep a box of baby wipes on hand while stamping. They are great for wiping off ink from edges of stamps, cleaning acrylic blocks before reusing and avoiding smudges made by inked fingers.
MELLETTE BEREZOWSKI

Colorize with Crayons

Stamp images onto **textured cardstock. Cut out images and color with crayons.** Choose a few subtle patterns/cardstock colors and cut into various sizes. Adhere stamped images and patterns/cardstock in a grid-like pattern on cardstock cut to 10" x 12". Place photo along side of collage. Adhere entire section to 12" x 12" background, adding a strip of scalloped paper. Finish off with journaling, accents and title.

Imagination at Play
By Jennifer J.

Acrylic stamps, paper, brads and stickers | AL
Ink | Tsukineko
Software | Adobe Photoshop CS2

Stamp on Book Papers

First Christmas
By Becky

Tear green cardstock and adhere to black background. Adhere photo and strips of red and black patterned paper. Add a strip of ledger paper to the top for a border. **Stamp Christmas trees onto book pages and patterned paper. Cut out and glue to bottom edge of layout. Stamp holly onto paper; cut out and color in leaves and berries.** Adhere tags to left of photo, then apply a frame rub-on, and stamp part of title inside. Hand write the rest above frame.

Ink | StazOn
Paper, stamps and embellishments | AL
Pens | Zig

Stamp with Solvent Ink

Imagination
By Robyn

Stitch blocks of polka dot paper and green paper to brown background. Affix photo and journaling strip on top. **Stamp on microscope slides with brown StazOn ink and various colors of paint.** Embellish with buttons and brads. Adhere to left side along with other patterned papers.

Acrylic stamps, button and microscope slides | AL
Font | 2Peas Gimme Coffee
Ink | Tsukineko
Paint | Delta and MM
Paper | My Mind's Eye and Chatterbox

Stamping on Cardboard

Cardboard Tags
By Jackie

Cut 2″ x 3″ tags from corrugated cardboard. **Using black StazOn ink, stamp flower images on each tag and let dry.** Add color to some of the flowers and petals using watercolors. Embellish tags with brads, buttons, gemstone brads for flower centers, small letter stickers for greetings and a ribbon.

Acrylic stamps and buttons | AL
Brads | AL and Lasting Impressions
Clip | EK Success
Ink | Tsukineko
Paint | Angora
Ribbon | SW and May Arts
Stickers | MM

How can I ensure I have enough ink on my stamp but not too much either?

Cathy Blackstone: Always place the stamp rubber-side up, flat on a hard surface like a desk. Dab ink onto the stamp surface. The application will then be even, and you will be able to see if you have missed any areas.

How can I keep my stamped image from smearing?

Mellette Berezowski: Press stamp firmly onto paper and avoid rocking the stamp, which often causes smearing or a halo effect.

I love to use acrylic paint in my projects, and I find myself using this most frequently with my acrylic stamps. There are two ways to use paint with your stamps—one messy and one not so messy! For the messy, squeeze a little bit of paint onto your index finger and swipe it all over the stamp. This method is also easy and fun to get two different colors onto your stamp to work into the design. Swipe part of it in one color, clean your finger on a baby wipe and then fill in the other part of your stamp in another color paint. The not so messy way is to use a foam brush to dip into your paint, and paint over the stamp.   EMILY FALCONBRIDGE

When I stamp with white StazOn (solvent ink) onto cardstock, it looks dull.

Patricia Anderson: StazOn is a solvent ink which is designed to work on slick, non-porous surfaces such as metal, glass, plastic, acrylic, transparencies and photos. Because the ink is absorbed by the paper, it appears dull. Use archival and pigment ink (must be heat set) on cardstock, and use solvent ink on items listed above to get the brightness you're after.

Stamp with Metallic Paint

To make the snowman card, clear emboss snowflakes on a circle card front. Add glitter glue on top and let dry. Cut out snowman, use a ribbon for the scarf and adhere to card. **Stamp heart with metallic paint, let dry, cut out, then embroider onto snowman.** Use black brads for eyes and nose.

For the star card, cut a large star and stamp with swirl stamp and metallic gold paint. When dry, adhere to card and machine stitch around the outside. Add greeting.

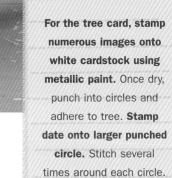

For the tree card, stamp numerous images onto white cardstock using metallic paint. Once dry, punch into circles and adhere to tree. **Stamp date onto larger punched circle.** Stitch several times around each circle.

Holiday Cards
By Cathy

Acrylic stamps | AL
Font | Blackmoor LET Plain
Ribbon | KI

seattle

shopgirls

$24.50

$29.50

the great thing about being the "american" cousin is when your canadian family wants to spend the weekend shopping with you...

OLD NAVY
395667-00-2
0002

Seattle Shopgirls
By Jennifer P.

Layer background with patterned paper and newsprint; adhere photos on top. **Using chalk inks, stamp images onto the newsprint. Carefully outline the images with a fine-tip pen.** Journal on stamped lines. Wrap twine around photos to attach a cluster of tags and adhere to page. Stamp date on white cardstock, cut out and adhere to bottom right side of page. Cut out letters for part of title.

Acrylic stamps | AL
Font | Clarendon and Shell
Ink | Clearsnap and Tsukineko
Paper | SW and SEI
Pens | Sakura
Software | Adobe Illustrator and Photoshop

Colorize with Watercolors

Claire and Kristen
By Kelli

Mat blue cardstock on white background. Ink edges of the white background cardstock and the photo; adhere photo to layout. **Stamp several images onto white cardstock. When ink is dry, watercolor in each stamped item.** Cut around each image, leaving a small white border. Cover photo with scrap paper and gently splatter blue paint around page. Affix stamped images to layout with pop dots. Use bookplate stamp to frame names.

Acrylic stamps | AL
Ink | Tsukineko
Paint | Crayola
Pens | AC

Stamp on Fabric

The Good Life
By Mellette

Zigzag stitch torn patterned paper to background. Print journaling on blue cardstock, round the edges and mat on white; adhere to background. **Stamp flowers and leaves on a fabric frame with pigment ink. Heat to set.** Frame photo mounted with foam tape and add metal corners and hinge to frame. Create title with foam and rub-on letters. Embellish layout with rub-ons, ribbon and clip.

Acrylic stamps | AL
Die cuts and hinge | MM
Font | Dustimo Roman
Ink | Stampin' Up!
Paper clip | Nunn Design
Paper | AL and SEI
Photo corners | Kolo
Ribbon | Masterpiece Studios
Rub-ons | BG, AC and Chatterbox
Stickers and Pens | AC

Winter Wonders
By Patricia

Adhere white scalloped paper to beige paper. Machine stitch a block of patterned paper over white paper. Cut red cardstock into a curve and attach along with photos. **Stamp title and snowflake border onto transparency using white solvent ink; adhere and tuck under** photos. **Stamp "Let it Snow" on a transparency with black solvent ink; cut out, color in with markers and attach with a gem brad. Stamp snowflakes randomly around page,** hand stitch over the top and use a brad for the center. **Stamp journaling stamp onto white cardstock, cut out, add journaling and affix to layout.**

Acrylic stamps | AL
Ink | StazOn
Paper | World Win Papers and AL
Pens | Sakura
Stamps and gem brads | AL

Stamp on a Transparency

Colorize with Pencil Crayons

Sunshine
By Robyn

Stamp sunshine circle stamp on yellow and blue cardstock with brown ink. Cut into a circle. Color in image on yellow with colored pencils. **Stamp other circle images with yellow and white paint and cut into circles.** Cut the insides from some circles and adhere around layout. Add stitching, buttons, brads, thread, etc. to embellish. **Stamp initial on transparency with yellow paint. When dry, stamp over it with silver glitter paint.**

Acrylic stamps and buttons | AL
Brads | Around the Block
Font | AL Uncle Charles
Ink | Stampin' Up!
Metal tag and clip | MM
Paint | MM and Deco Art
Paper Frill | Doodlebug Designs
Paper | AL and Gartner Studios

You definitely have us all wrapped around your finger, that's obvious.

But what is so cool is that you do it to everyone you meet. You amaze them with your sweet words, melt them with your sweet smile.

little **Charmer**

Whether it's family that we don't see often, or new teachers or friends, you hook them in right away and leave a special spot in their heart.

caleb vobb
Ventura
Summer
2006

Charmer
By Jamie

Acrylic stamps | AL
Brads | AC
Ink | Stampin' Up!
Paper | AC and AL
Transparency | Hambly

Mat photo on cardstock and leave left side untrimmed for labels. Adhere to layout, slipping patterned paper behind photos. Affix labels in a row. **Stamp photo corners on patterned paper and cut out. Hand write journaling on labels and stamp title. Apply labels to the top of layout, stamp image on top and add brads.**

Techniques & Fun Stuff

Do you hem and haw at the scrapbook store debating whether or not to buy a stamp, wondering if you'll get enough use out of it? Don't wait any longer—just buy it! These artists have jumped out of the box and explored how versatile these clear stamps are. Be ready to be amazed by Jamie's stamped silk flower accents, Emily's use of the journaling blocks as a title background and Jennifer's skill at turning a stamped image into a computer brush for a digital layout. You'll also be impressed by how bleach can make an image stand out or how walnut ink can give a stamped image a super cool look. Now just take these ladies' lead, **roll up your sleeves and get stamping!**

Scrap Friends
By Emily

Paint acrylic onto journaling stamps and stamp onto white cardstock. When dry, cut out and roughen edges. Layer onto page and use as a background for page title.

Acrylic stamps | AL
Chipboard | Advantus
Paint | Derivan Matisse
Pens | Sharpie and AC
Rub-ons | MM

Stamp Journaling Blocks

A Card to Match Your Layout

Walnut Inked Cards
By Cathy

Clear emboss images onto cards. Spray walnut ink onto cards and let sit. **The stamped images will act as a "pool" to the ink allowing the ink to dry darker within the images.** Cut rectangles from felt, spray with liquid adhesive and sprinkle with glitter. Stitch to card and adhere stamped sentiments on top.

Acrylic stamps and walnut ink | AL
Embossing powder | Hero Arts
Glitter | Glitterex Corp.
Ink | Tsukineko

How do I apply glitter to my stamped images?

Robyn Werlich: An easy way to apply glitter to an entire image is to stamp an image with Mod Podge. Apply the glue to the stamp, stamp on paper, then sprinkle the glitter on the image. Let the glitter sit for a bit before sprinkling off the excess glitter. Be sure to wash the stamp quickly after. To apply glitter to a small portion of the stamp, stamp with regular ink on cardstock. Use a liquid glue to outline or color in a spot on the stamped image. Sprinkle glitter, let sit, then brush off the remaining glitter.

Stamping has quickly become one of my favorite "tools" for scrapbooking. It is fun, easy and creative. Every time I pull out a stamp, I have a new way I want to use it. I love how freeing the process is. There is no limit; if I don't like it, I just try something else! These clear stamps make the whole process of creating so enjoyable. They store so nicely, are easy to go through and easy to clean and put away. I find myself reaching for my stamps on almost every layout I do these days!

JENNIFER JOHNER

Resist with Walnut Ink

so far....my very favorite picture of you

summer 2006

Brynn

When embossing a stamped image, how do I know when I've heated it long enough?

If the image looks a bit "greasy" after embossing, you have heated it too long. If it looks grainy, you need to heat it longer. You should have a nice, clean, raised image when finished.

Clear emboss images onto background. Spray walnut ink on top and let sit. When dry, paint a background for photo, then add thin strips of paper around the edges. Hand stitch around the outside of the layout.

Brynn
By Cathy

Acrylic stamps, walnut ink and letter stickers | AL Gems | Westrim

Create a Stamped Pattern

Acrylic stamps | AL
Die cuts | Sassafrass Lass and KI
Font | Helvetica Light 45
Ink | Clearsnap and Tsukineko

Paper | Chatterbox
Punches | EK Success
Ribbon | AC
Stickers | SEI

Fall in Love   By Jennifer P.

Place photos, papers and embellishments onto background. Once you have a general idea of where the items will be placed, remove all items from background paper. **Using chalk ink, stamp leaf image across the page. Stamp dots around the leaves in a contrasting color. Finish the pattern by adding flourish stamps in a wave pattern along the bottom edge of the paper.** Adhere photos, papers and embellishments to page.

When embossing with powders, pour the powder over a coffee filter. It's easy to fold into a funnel to pour the remaining powder back into your container, and coffee filters are cheap and disposable!

JENNIFER PEBBLES

thinking of you.

Acrylic stamps | AL
Embossing powder | Stampendous
Fabric tabs/circles | 7gypsies
Ink | Clearsnap and Tsukineko
Paper | BG
Punches | EK Success
Ribbon | May Arts

especially for you!

happy day !

Spotlight Tags
By Jackie

Cut tags from kraft cardstock and add strips/blocks of patterned paper. **Stamp images on the kraft portion of the tags using brown ink and VersaMark ink embossed with clear powder. Stamp an extra of each image onto coordinating cardstock with a different ink color.** Punch a circle for the extra images and using a pop dot, mount them over the images that were stamped on the kraft. Embellish tags with fabric reinforcements, ribbon and a small greeting strip attached with a staple.

Accent Stamped Images

What is "kissing" in stamping terms?

Robyn Werlich: "Kissing" your stamps is a really fun technique. Take a bold stamp and add a pattern to it with another stamp. First, apply ink to a bold stamp. Then using a stamp that has a pattern on it, press it down on the inked stamp. It will remove the ink from the bold stamp to create a pattern. Stamp onto cardstock. For a two-tone effect, ink patterned stamp in a different color before placing it on top of the inked bold image.

Stamp a Background Paper

Acrylic stamps and die cuts | AL
Brad and photo corner | MM
Journaling spots | Advantus
Paper | AL and CI
Pens | AC
Photo turn | 7gypsies
Ribbon | May Arts
Stickers | AL, Chatterbox, Heidi Grace Designs, Bo Bunny, Creative Imagination and 7gypsies

Kindergarten
By Mellette

Trim red cardstock to 11⅜" x 12". Stitch a large piece of blue cardstock to right side of red paper and add white scalloped paper on top. **Stamp numbers and letters on white paper.** Mat large photo on yellow patterned paper. Mat smaller photo with green and adhere slightly overlapping large photo. Use chipboard and letter stickers to create title across bottom of large photo. Write journaling on journaling spots and adhere below large photo.

Stamp on Fabric Flowers

a.m.
By Jamie

Mat photo on ledger paper. Trim off edge of scalloped cardstock and add to top of ledger paper. **Stamp on flowers and attach with brads. Stamp title onto ledger paper and add brad brackets.** Hand write journaling and add sticker embellishments.

Acrylic stamps | AL
Brads | Around the Block
Flowers | Prima
Paper | Fontwerks and Scenic Route
Pens | AC
Stickers | 7gypsies and KI

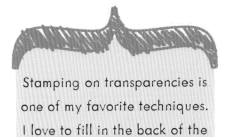

Stamping on transparencies is one of my favorite techniques. I love to fill in the back of the image with paint, markers, fabric, patterned paper, etc.
PATRICIA ANDERSON

Stamp on Buttons

Grama
By Jennifer J.

Cover black background with a large piece of patterned paper. Layer an enlarged photo on top. **Stamp flowers and cut out.** Place around photo and machine stitch circles in the center to secure to page. **Stamp on buttons and use as flower centers.** Cut journaling into strips and adhere to page.

Acrylic stamps, buttons and paper | AL
Ink | Tsukineko
Photo | Dawn Graham
Software | Adobe Photoshop CS2

Use Shrink Plastic

Space Tags
By Jackie

Cut three different cards from white cardstock and add lines, swooshes and freehanded rings of patterned papers. **Stamp images onto white, clear and black shrink film using black StazOn and white pigment ink. Cut or punch film into shapes and punch a regular-sized hole into each.** Shrink film according to manufacturer's directions. Once cool, add color to the charms using pencil crayons or Sharpie markers. Attach charms to card faces using hemp cording or brads; finish with small greetings or quotes.

Acrylic stamp | AL
Brads | American Tag
Font | 2Peas Crazy Dreams
Ink | Tsukineko and Inkadinkadoo
Markers | Sharpie
Paper | AL, KI and BG

One of the reasons I love AL clear stamps is because well... they're clear! Sometimes when I'm stamping, if I haven't inked well enough, a little piece of the image will be missing or won't be as clear as the rest. I love the clear stamps because I can re-ink and re-stamp the missed portion. Because the stamps are clear, I can see exactly where to stamp!
PATRICIA ANDERSON

Q&a

How could you use watercolors to fill in a stamped image?

Jackie Bonette: Watercolors can be used in a few different ways to add nice, soft color to an image. For one, stamp image in waterproof ink, let dry and then using a paintbrush and watercolor paints, fill in image where desired with color. Color in the image can be diluted somewhat by pulling the color around in the image with a wet brush (no paint).

Another idea is when using a water-based ink, stamp the image and then pull the ink into other blank areas of the image just by using a wet brush. Finally, there are great watercolor pencils on the market. Again, stamp an image with waterproof ink, let dry and then using the pencils, color in the image as desired. When finished, use a blender pen or slightly wet paintbrush to dilute and spread the penciled colors. All of these techniques work best with a good weight, textured cardstock to help prevent warping and curling.

Cut Out Stamped Letters

Trim one side from scalloped paper and attach to dot background paper; adhere blue and red cardstock next to scalloped paper. Cover seam with ribbon. **Stamp letter stamps on patterned paper.** Cut letters apart and attach below photo. Secure with stitching, staples, brads and buttons. Add rub-ons as desired. Hand write journaling inside a stamped journaling circle.

My Boys
By Mellette

Ink | Clearsnap
Paper, die cuts, stickers, stamps, buttons, brads, ribbon and rub-ons | AL
Pens | AC

Cut Out Stamped Images

Spring
By Jennifer J.

Font | 2Peas Secret Pal
Ink | StazOn
Jewels | Advantus
Paper | AL, Sassafras Lass, My Mind's Eye and BG
Software | Adobe Photoshop CS2
Stamps | AL

Adhere assorted sizes of patterned paper and a photo to green scalloped paper, then adhere all over black background. **Stamp butterfly image on various patterned papers; cut out. Adhere butterflies to layout and hand stitch a trail for one butterfly. Stamp in layers directly over photo to create the title.** Print white text in a black box, cut into strips and affix to page. Adhere jewels on the butterflies and journaling strips.

Stitch over Stamped Images

Cousins
By Jennifer J.

Adhere an enlarged photo to background, then add a chipboard shape and rub-ons. **Stamp title and star images.** Machine stitch over title and stars. (Using the backstitch function makes it easier to maneuver around the curved letters.) Machine stitch along the bottom and adhere journaling cut into strips.

Acrylic stamps, chipboard, paper and rub-ons | AL
Ink | Tsukineko

Stamp on Fabric

Nine Months
By Patricia

Cut several patterned papers and adhere to gold background paper. **Adhere photos and stamp design onto center photo. Stamp birds onto fabric and cut out bodies. Stamp birds onto a transparency, cut out and adhere over fabric. Stamp flower petals and word "love" onto fabric, cut around design and affix to page. Stamp clear buttons with flower centers, back with green patterned paper, tie with thread and adhere to page. Print "9 Months" onto a transparency, stamp tab around words, cut out and secure to page.**

Font | AL Delight and AL Uncle Charles
Ink | StazOn
Paper | AL and K&Co.
Stamps | AL

3 Dimensional Images

Explore. Dream. Discover.
By Mellette

Acrylic stamps and stickers | AL
Die cuts | Heidi Grace Designs
Paper | AL, My Mind's Eye and Sandylion
Pens | AC
Ribbon, crystal brads and photo corner | MM
Software | Adobe Photoshop Elements
Stick pin | Heidi Grace Designs

Layer strips of patterned paper to background. Scallop bottom edge. Fold wide yellow ribbon and pull a small amount of fold through a metal washer and add a decorative pin. Staple ribbon to left side. Print title on a 5" x 7" photo. **Stamp flourish clear stamps around photo.** Machine stitch a curve on layout three to four times with dark brown thread. **Stamp butterflies along stitching. Stamp butterflies again onto various patterned papers. For each butterfly stamped on layout, stamp two more on patterned paper.** Cut out butterflies — except the antennae — from patterned papers. Matching up stamped images on layout, glue one cutout of each butterfly directly over the stamped image. For the second set of butterflies, gently fold in half and apply adhesive only to the center back portion of the butterfly. Adhere and gently push wings of butterflies slightly upward to give them dimension.

Scan and Enlarge

Super Hubby
By Jennifer P.

Stamp image on white paper with black ink. Scan image into computer editing program; refine and resize image as desired. Define Brush to create computer "stamp." Open new file to desired size, stamp image onto new layer with Brush Tool, adjusting color and angle as preferred. Print page and add embellishments, stamps and photos.

Acrylic stamp | AL
Brads | Queen & Co.
Font | Helvetica Light 45
Ink | Clearsnap
Paper and stamps | AL
Ribbon | May Arts, AC and MM
Software | Adobe Photoshop CS2
Stickers | Doodlebug Designs
Tags | SW

Bleach Stamping

Hi Princess
By Robyn

Brush alphabet stamps with bleach. Stamp onto red cardstock. Stamp "HI" onto pink cardstock using bleach and stitch inside the "I". Adhere in place with mounting tape. (Quickly clean off stamps with soap and water.) Adhere matted photo and journaling to right side of layout. Embellish the side of the photo with flowers, brads, clear buttons, metal heart, etc. Add metal trim and blue paper fringe across the bottom.

Acrylic stamps and buttons | AL
Flowers | AC
Font | AL Lean Tower
Metal heart, trim and brads | MM
Paper | Lasting Impressions and Doodlebug Designs
Silhouette word | Advantus

Stamping Gallery

"Creativity is a continual surprise." Author Ray Bradbury was right on with his observation. When artists are given various tools and supplies, it's always a pleasant surprise to see what they'll create. Peruse these pages and **be surprised** at how versatile clear stamps can be and what these ladies can fashion when they are set free and have no rules.

Combine Several Techniques on One Page

Acrylic stamps and chipboard star | AL
Brad | MM
Die cuts | Sizzix, Quickutz and AL
Font | AL Uncle Charles
Ink | Tsukineko
Paper | AL and My Mind's Eye
Pens and embossing powder | Stampin' Up!
Rub-ons | My Mind's Eye

Stamp various stars on several surfaces (fabric, vellum, cardstock, transparency, etc.). Heat emboss some with embossing powder. Cut out each star. Cover a chipboard star with embossing ink and sprinkle with silver embossing powder. Heat to create a silver star. Affix stars to background. Stamp title onto cork and outline each letter with a brown marker.

Play
By Robyn

Try Flocking Powder

Adored
By Robyn

Brush white paint on flower stamp and stamp onto green, blue and yellow cardstocks. When dry, apply 2-way liquid glue to center of stamped images. Quickly sprinkle with blue or white flocking powder and push down into the glue. Let sit, then sprinkle off the remaining powder. **Stamp label stamps on patterned paper, cut out and tuck under the main photo.**

Acrylic stamps and die cuts | AL
Flocking powder | Stampendous
Flowers and brads | MM
Paper | Lasting Impressions and BG
Pens | Stampin' Up!

Trees
By Cathy

For "What's Up?", **stamp leaves onto white cardstock and cut out.** Adhere to top of cut-out tree. Assemble, then attach tree to card. Embellish with stitching and a rub-on greeting.

To make "Love, Enjoy, Laugh," create tree by using two different shades of orange cardstock that have been distressed around the edges. **Stamp bird onto pink patterned paper and also onto white and yellow cardstock.** Cut the body of the bird out of the pink, the beak out of the yellow and the legs out of white cardstock. Assemble and adhere to top of tree. Embellish with words cut out from patterned paper, sequins and stitching around the outside of the tree.

Acrylic stamps | AL
Ink | Clearsnap and Tsukineko
Paper | BG and K&Co.
Rub-ons | KI and AL
Sequin | Westrim

For "Hi," **stamp two different flower images onto green and white cardstock.** When dry, punch images from cardstock using a small circle punch. Assemble tree and machine stitch circles around each stamped image.

Be Who You Are
By Leslie

To make clay accents, roll out colored clay to ¼″ thickness. **Using a dry stamp image (stars) press firmly into clay. Lightly brush metallic gold chalk over the surface of the stamped clay to highlight the raised areas.** Bake the clay on a cookie sheet lined with waxed paper at 250 degrees fahrenheit for 15 minutes (or as directed on package). Adhere to layout with Diamond Glaze. Stamp stars onto white cardstock with black ink. Brush over the image with metallic gold chalk to give color to the stamped image.

Stamp Into Clay

DO NOT leave stamps sitting in water overnight—they are never the same. They turn whitish, get tacky and lose their shape a bit.

KELLI CROWE

Acrylic Stamps | AL
Font | Kirby and Impact
Jumbo photo corner | 7gypsies
Paper and ribbon | KI

Create Clever Card Designs

Skinny Flower Cards
By Cathy

Cut and fold 1½" x 12" strips of kraft cardstock. **Stamp petals using three different shades of pink onto white cardstock; cut out. Stamp flower centers onto dark brown cardstock, punch out, then adhere to metal-rimmed tag. Stamp and cut out leaves and stems.** Assemble flowers onto folded card and embellish with jewels and a printed greeting.

Acrylic stamps | AL
Font | 2Peas Frappuchino
Ink | Clearsnap and Tsukineko
Jewels | Westrim

Stamp on Vellum

Date Tags
By Cathy

Stamp date stamp onto natural colored cardstock; let dry, then check and circle the appropriate dates. Adhere to cardstock, cut out and round corners. Print greetings onto vellum, then place vellum over the stamped card, making sure greeting is in correct place. Sandwich ribbon between two layers and stitch all layers together with a zigzag stitch. Add button on top of ribbon.

Acrylic stamps and ribbon | AL
Font | AL Broken
Ink | Tsukineko

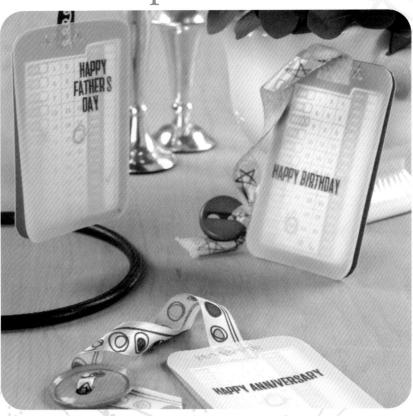

Create a Stamped Collage

Flower Tags
By Jackie

Make tag bases from cardstock and patterned paper. **Stamp flower image in several colors onto kraft cardstock;** trim close to image. Cut out an imperfect circle and secure to the center with a brad. **Stamp greeting onto an index card,** cut out, round the corners and staple to tag. Punch a hole at the top and add a binder ring tied with ribbon.

Acrylic stamps | AL
Brads | AC and SEI
Ink | Tsukineko and Clearsnap
Paper | AL and MM
Pens | Zig
Ribbon | May Arts and Michaels

Stamp a Clay Accent

Acrylic stamps | AL
Book plate | 7gypsies
Ink | Tsukineko
Modeling clay | Sculpty
Paper | AL and 7gypsies
Pens | AC
Photo | Tara Whitney

Mat square photo onto blue paper; tear around the edges. Add black strips around all sides. To make the title, spread out clay about ⅛" thick onto a flat surface. **Press the stamp into the clay. Shape two hearts out of the clay. Bake for about 10 minutes, following manufacturer's directions.** Adhere the hearts and the title with glue dots. Ink the edges of mini tags and hand write journaling. Adhere small hand cut and inked circles from red paper and corrugated black paper along with the tags. Adhere the book plate over the dried clay with glue dots.

I Heart You   By Kelli

I really like to incorporate vintage book pages and ledger bits on my layouts. The AL stamps are perfect for this. I just stamp on my vintage pieces and cut them out to add just a touch of my personality without overwhelming the page.   BECKY NOVACEK

Basic Stamping

Creative Always
By Jackie

Stamp flower image several times onto white cardstock in a couple of different ink colors. When dry, trim close to image, even trimming off some edges of the actual image. Adhere photos onto background. Tear a piece of fabric, spray with adhesive and adhere to bottom corner of layout. Finish layout by adding the stamped images, a small ribbon tab, staples and journaling.

Ink | Clearsnap
Stamps and ribbon | AL

Cut Out Stamped Images

Play Hard
By Jackie

Stamp circle word images onto corrugated cardboard and cardstock. Trim into circles. Add colored center on one, hand journal on another and back a third with red cardstock. Create bottom portion of layout by lining up strips of patterned papers and ribbon. Hand stitch over ribbon with hemp. Sew on a row of black buttons, to mimic wheels, using waxed linen.

Ink | Memories
Paper | My Mind's Eye, Scenic Route and CI
Ribbon | Michaels
Stamps and buttons | AL

Resist an Image

Always Forever
By Leslie

Using black pigment ink, stamp images onto white glossy paper. Emboss the black stamped image with clear embossing powder. Using a pink inkpad, rub color onto the stamped image. Embellish stamped images with rhinestones.

Acrylic stamps | AL
Font | Kaufmann Bd BT
Ink | Hero Arts
Paper | AL, DMD and SEI
Rhinestones | Westrim
Velvet trim | Fancy Pants

Stamp into Dimensional Paste

Truly Amazing
By Leslie

Sloppily apply a thick layer of dimensional green paint onto white cardstock. **Stamp into the paint with a clear stamp.** Set aside to dry and then crop into a rectangle. **To make the stamped chipboard circles, press a small flower stamp into a white pigment inkpad so there is excess ink on the stamp. Press the flower image onto small chipboard circles.** Sprinkle with embossing enamel and heat emboss. Press the entire circle into VersaMark inkpad and apply embossing enamel two more times. **Stamp title and calendar stamp on white cardstock with black dye ink.** Cut out and add to page.

Acrylic stamps and twill | AL
Chipboard circles | Bazzill
Font | Dyspepsia
Heart accents | Westrim
Index tab | 7gypsies
Ink | Tsukineko
Paper | AL, DMD and Basic Grey
Photo corner | Daisy D's
Tag | K&Co

Repeat the Same Stamp

Cool
By Jennifer J.

Adhere patterned paper to kraft background. **Stamp same image on four colors of cardstock; cut out.** Cut assorted sizes of patterned paper that coordinate with the cardstock. Adhere stamping blocks and patterned paper to form a "rainbow" alongside the photo. Journal on the stamped journaling blocks. **For the stamping below the photo, only ink part of the stamp.** Finish off with embellishments and title.

Acrylic stamp and buttons | AL
Flowers | Bazzill
Ink | StazOn
Paper | AL, Sassafras Lass and BG
Pens | Uniball
Photo credits | Dawn Graham
Software | Adobe Photoshop CS2
Stickers | AC

Try the Resist Technique

Create background from horizontal and vertical strips of patterned paper. **For the numbers at the bottom, stamp numbers onto white cardstock with VersaMark ink and then emboss with embossing enamel. Using a sponge and green ink, swipe over the cardstock and numbers.** Highlight the number "2" with a circle frame, machine stitching and hand stitching. Trim photos and other accents into squares and round the corners.

2 Silly
By Mellette

Acrylic stamps and clip | AL
Die cuts | AL, KI and Imagination Project
Rub-ons | Fancy Pants
Ink | Tsukineko and Stampin' Up!
Paper | Imagination Project and AL
Ribbon | MM and KI
Stickers | Advantus, Heidi Grace Design, Cloud 9 Design, AL and Kelly Panicci
Pearl brad | K&Co.
Flowers | Prima
Pens | AC

Stamp on Paper Bags

Baby Tags and Bags
By Jackie

Stamp tiny paper bag fronts with greeting. For the carriage, stamp image on cardstock, trim and adhere. Cut small card enclosures from index cards and add a few small stamped background images. Add a small ribbon tie fastened with a tiny safety pin.

Acrylic stamps | AL
Ink | Clearsnap
Ribbon | May Arts and Michaels
Safety pins | MM

How do I keep my inkpads from drying out?

Mellette Berezowski: Store your inkpads upside down and use a re-inker over pads as necessary.

Stamp on Glass Slides

Superstar Kid
By Mellette

Adhere blocks of patterned paper to white cardstock, then mount entire piece on black. **For the title background, use a piece of white felt to stamp alcohol inks onto microscope slide covers;** let dry. Adhere stamped slide covers at top of page with white craft glue. **Stamp title on top with StazOn.** Finish layout with ribbon, photos, journaling and chipboard accents.

Acrylic stamps | AL
Die cuts | AL and KI
Ink | Tsukineko and Ranger
Microscope slide | VWR Scientific Inc.
Paper | AL and Carolee's Creations
Pens | AC
Photo | Winnie Fink and Life Touch
Ribbon | MM

Stamp Page Accents

Refresh
By Jennifer P.

Stamp images with paint onto cardstock. Allow to dry. Cut assorted patterned paper into various sizes and cut stamped cardstock into several sizes. Adhere shapes onto background paper along with photo. **Stamp flower images onto kraft cardstock and cut out. Complete layout with stamped accents, buttons, title, journaling and machine stitching.**

Acrylic stamps, buttons and chipboard | AL
Cord | Advantus
Ink | Ranger
Paper | AL and My Mind's Eye

> I love the versatility of the stamps because they look completely different if I use them with ink or paint, on cardstock or patterned paper. KELLI CROWE

Stamp a Border

Us Right Now
By Emily

Paint a rectangle onto patterned paper background. **When dry, repeatedly stamp the same image around the edge of the paint to form a border. Add dots of glitter to stamped image.** Journal on painted background with a white pen. Hand stitch around photos for interest.

Acrylic stamps and paper | AL
Ink | Ranger
Paint | Derivan Matisse
Pen | Uniball
Stickers | 7gypsies

priceless

Emboss with Glitter

delight

May you always **delight**
In the simple things of life.

Grow strong Madisyn,

Grow **beautifully**…

just like you are!

Brush decoupage medium onto stamp and quickly stamp onto patterned paper. Sprinkle with fine glitter and shake off excess. Let dry. Repeat with various stamps, patterned papers and colors of glitter to create the flower petals. Spray petals with matte finishing spray to protect and seal the glitter. Assemble base of layout with cardstock, photo and ribbon. Adhere flowers to layout and machine stitch the stems.

Delight
By Robyn

Acrylic stamps | AL
Die cuts | Advantus
Font | AL Uncle Charles and Susie's Hand
Paper | Lasting Impressions and Chatterbox
Ribbon and metal letter | MM

Combine Techniques & Materials

Lake Powell
By Robyn

Layer background with patterned paper, eyelet trim and photos. For heart embellishment, cover a large chipboard heart with polka dot paper. Adhere two thin strips of red paper down the middle. **Stamp journaling lines with StazOn ink on transparency.** Back with yellow cardstock and staple to left side of heart. **Stamp images onto various papers, cut to size and adhere to right side.** Embellish with brads.

Acrylic stamps | AL
Die cuts | Jenni Bowlin Studio, Quickutz and Cuttlebug
Font | AL Uncle Charles
Ink | Stampin' Up! and Tsukineko
Paper | Lasting Impressions, Scenic Route, MM, My Mind's Eye and BG
Pens | Stampin' Up!

Colorize Stamps

Ivy Art
By Emily

Stamp title onto white cardstock with black ink. Color in the letters with watercolor pencils, then with a fine-tip paintbrush, dip the brush in water and paint over the pencil. Adhere photos and artwork. Create a background for the entire page by coloring and painting over with water.

Acrylic stamps | AL
Ink | Ranger and Derivan Matisse
Jewels | Advantus

Stamp on Buttons

Summer

By Jamie

Stamp images onto clear buttons using StazOn ink. Swipe the back of the buttons with colored ink. Stitch buttons to kraft cardstock. Mat photo on patterned paper and affix to cardstock. Use letter stickers and handwriting for the title. **Stamp journaling lines and hand write journaling. Stamp scroll frame image and cut in half; adhere to top and bottom of journaling block.**

long entwining days of
summer

Three months off from school ... long days together ... it all meshes together as the long days go by. You get bored, you have fun. TOGETHER!
summer 2006

Acrylic stamps | AL
Buttons | 7gypsies
Ink | Tsukineko and Stampin' Up!
Paper | Mustard Moon and KI
Pens and stickers | AC

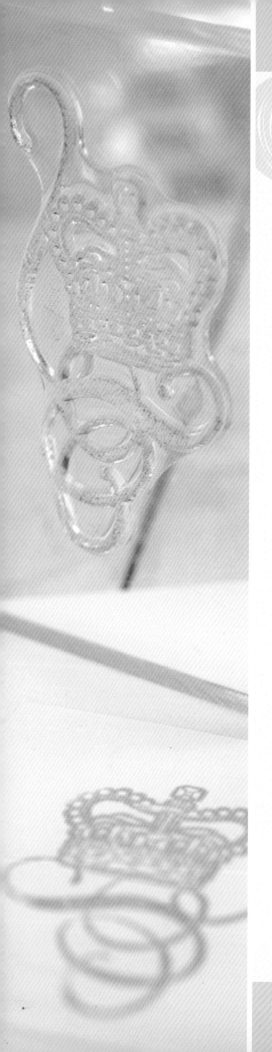

Q&A

I want to get into stamping, but I don't have a large stash of tools or supplies. Can I get started without the expense of buying everything at once?

Jennifer Johner: Of course! This is one of the things that kept me away from stamping. I always thought it was cool but didn't have all of the stuff I knew was available. But you know what? I still don't! My collection consists of stamps and a few different colors of ink. Most of the time I find that I stamp mostly in black!

Do I have to wash stamps after every use?

Becky Novacek: Yes. I keep baby wipes by my stamps for easy cleanup. I also have a small wire basket near my desk where I toss really inky stamps that need more than a quick wipe. At the end of my scrapping time, I wash them all at once.

My kids always want to use my stamps. How can I get them involved?

Kelli Crowe: It is great to get the kids involved in stamping. They enjoy it and it is a great exercise for fine motor skills. They can stamp in ink and then color in the image with crayons, colored pencils or markers. My boys enjoy making up stories inspired by the stamps and turning them into little books. My youngest loves to wash the stamps when we are done.

How do I prepare my stamps for use?

Leslie Lightfoot: Acrylic stamps have a coating on them when you first open the package. Wash them a few times or rub the stamp on paper to remove the coating. This will keep the ink that you apply from bubbling on the surface.

How do I store these clear stamps?

Jamie Waters: The easy clam shell packaging is a breeze to use and store. I love how I can see my images without having to open up each package. I love how they are so thin and I can stack them in a tub without taking up too much space. The way they cling to the sheet once I clean them off is genius! Now instead of throwing them all over my desk, I can't help but put them back where they belong.